W9-CIQ-498

* *

Thank God
for
the red,
white and black

* *

* * * * * * * * * * * * * * * * * * *

Thank God
for
the red,
white and black

* * * * * * * * * * * * * * * * * *

by
Jeanette Struchen

J. B. LIPPINCOTT COMPANY
Philadelphia & New York

★ ★ ★ ★ ★ ★ ★ ★ ★

For Don

★ ★ ★ ★ ★ ★ ★ ★ ★

Introduction

For me

Prayer is discovery of new depths, not the practice of new techniques.

Prayer-powerful is, for me, prayer-simple.

Prayer is freedom—to say whatever I want however I want, or to say nothing at all—with the assurance of being understood.

Prayer is a mood, not a posture. It may be as worthwhile at the kitchen sink as in church.

Prayer is belief that someone is listening. I can believe in God and not pray, but I cannot pray disbelieving in God.

—*Jeanette Struchen*

* * * * * * * * * * * * * * * * * * * *

Thank God
for
the red,
white and black

* * * * * * * * * * * * * * * * * * * *

Three cheers for people in the resistance movement,
　　Lord.
For those who can resist
　　　　a bargain if they can't use it
　　　　a product if they don't like it
　　　　a style if they can't wear it
　　　　a compliment if they don't deserve it
　　　　a doctrine if they can't believe it
　　　　a spree if they can't afford it
　　　　a joke if they don't get it
　　　　a rumor if they can't swallow it
　　　　a war if they can't support it.

Lord, lead me into temptation—
    to say what I think
    to believe what I know
    to act what I feel.
I'm burning at the stake to be me.

Lord, we need a switched-on miracle.
A lot of people are starving
          and
     feeding them looks like a mission impossible.
We've studied them
     stared at them
          counted them
               organized them
                    collected for them
                         editorialized them
                              prayed for them
                              and
                                   buried them.
Now we need a few loaves, a couple of fish, and You.

Lord, there are a lot of people wanting to back up
    to a myth called the good old days.
What they mean is their shock absorbers are shot
        and
    they've freaked out in despair.
Was there really a time
    when the natives weren't restless?
    when the generation gap didn't show?
    when moral standards weren't being glued
        together?
    Rebellion started in the Garden of Eden,
    topless dancers entertained the Pharaohs
        and
    at least
    one rebellious youth was crucified.
Once in a while, Lord, it might be nice to drive
    around and rubberneck amid the good old days,
    but keep us from parking.

Lord, I've sat in this whale long enough.
    Let me out!
Inactivity breeds apathy
        and
I'm hypnotized by obsoletes.
    I hear that
        skin color is out and promise-pushing is in,
        poverty is out and crowing over the moon is in,
        marches are out and riots are in,
        fair-housing is out so neighbors are in.
    Next time around people may be out.
Something tells me man is strapped to a clock, Lord,
    and if we can't stop unwinding before the alarm
    goes off we'll all be back in trees.

Lord, can our national debt exceed our national guilt?
    Seems as though we've wrapped a lot in
    Indian blankets and gone out of our way to
    ignore smoke signals.

Seems as though we've thrown bombs without
    targets, knowing a well-aimed slingshot can
    level a giant.

    Seems as though we keep a finger in the dike
    when we might better keep a foot on the ark.

Lord, if confession of sins helps the drowning, hear us
    quick before man becomes a second Titanic.

Lord, help me brush up on people.

Some are square as ice cubes and as stuck in molds.

Some are self-winding in the mouth and content to be where the inaction is.

Some have diet-size consciences about king-size issues.

Some believe integration is a pilot experiment instead of a pivotal expedient to brotherhood.

Some get addicted to their own skin, forgetting we all came out of the cave the same color.

Lord, have you ever thought of letting man back in the Garden and starting over?

Thank God for ★ ★ ★

We're pussyfooting, Lord.
The whites are getting whiter and the colors bolder.
Is that storm over integration about to end in sheet
     lightning?
If so we may be on another detour through the
     Dark Ages.

Lord, as the halls of ivy shake I have to keep
sorting out whether the root of the problem lies in
plugged pipelines to the dean's office
           or
just our tired, our poor students yearning to breed
free.

Thank God for ★ ★ ★

Lord, most of us could use a "wonder" drug.
Wonder is scarce around here.
The only time I feel wonder is when somebody snaps
    the backside of the moon or when autumn
    saddles up for her annual show.
Maybe wonder is scarce because it's old-fashioned
    like charity or going the second mile.
All I know is that my house is full of gadgets and
    the office is full of computers but nothing is
    cracking my sound barrier.
I think a little wonder might do it.

God, I don't want to be the spitting image of
    anybody.
I'm a new breed ungullible but I feel like old General
    Custer surrounded by redskins.
I've copped out on taking the blame for leftover
    prejudice and bell-tower trivia.
Most people are using the surburban thing as a
    smoke screen for reality
        and
   you know, Lord, nobody over thirty buys reality.
Let the dead bury the dead;
I'm hitting the evacuation route.
Lord, I'm not running from change;
I'm running from the Dark Ages.
I'm not looking for rebellion;
I'm looking for new alternatives.
Listen, Lord, you said it yourself:
       "Let there be light."

I've just come from the plea market, **Lord.**
   There was a plea for money
      for better attendance
      for volunteers
      for old clothes
        and
      new folding chairs.
Once upon a time the standard package **plea**
      mentioned
         sin
         salvation
         and
         alcohol.
Is the fault in today's action, Lord, or in yesterday's
      decisions?

Special people, Lord, are like the beads of a rosary—each in a separate place but strung together as reminders that someone broke through and loved us.

She split the scene bag and baggage, Lord,
And on the way out swatted her parents with four-
letter words.
By shedding her cool she raised the master antenna
of every neighbor on the block
and
they've unanimously awarded her a badge of
infamy.
Wherever she is tonight she must be drained
and
if she isn't lonely she's faking it.
After she hangs loose awhile maybe her blinking
memory bank will lead her back.
But it takes more than tears of forgiveness to sew
up the generation gap.

Lord, at what point on the historical watershed will
man realize:
an eye for an eve leads to blindness, not better
vision,
soul-searching questions cannot be satisfied with
computer-programmed answers,
it was for the world, not the church, that You
gave Your Only,
the invitation was to come and follow an example, not
come worship a halo?
Such items may be worth remembering as man packs
his survival kit.

Thank God for ★ ★ ★

Lord, you were the original flower child suggesting
    that we consider the lilies.
If we had done it we wouldn't be out making
        hydrogen bombs
        napalm
        antimissile missiles
        nerve gas
          and
        nuclear submarines.
Thank you for the few people left who go to the
    garden to consider the dew on the roses.

Lord, how far can I fly a principle?
I've let out string to meet the winds of change
      but
    velocity is so strong I can't keep my feet on the
      ground.
Now I know why some people fly trial balloons in-
    stead of convictions.
    This is work, Lord.
    Principles demand attention.
    I could haul them in and tie them down
    Close my eyes and let them go
      or
    Hold tight and stand my ground.
Lord, is this one of the games people play?

For some of us the church is a hobby, Lord.
We can pick it up or lay it down
        but
        what we really want is out.
Everybody knows the church is choking
        from
        too much theological mumbo jumbo
        too many prepackaged affirmations
        and
        too few underground rebels.
Bless those people who are going over the wall
        to do their thing
        and
        bless the rest of us before we get hardening
        of the religious arteries.

O *God*, I'm like the boy at Qumran Cave who didn't
    know the value of his discovery.
I'm running in neutral instead of huffing and puffing
    to lift the world.
I'm too shockable and can't hang loose with the
    times.
I'll never lose my life for Your sake because I can't
    even shake my conscience.
I deny myself in bite sizes and cross-bearing is no
    more than noble hypocrisy.
    Am I Your betrayer?
    Is it I, Lord?
    Is it I?

I can't help laughing, Lord.
It's like a backdoor miracle
      and
    thank you thank you!
Someone has finally come along to shake man's con-
      science on
    racism
      bigotry
        hypocrisy
          war
            and
              conformity.
That someone is anybody in purple suspenders, long
    hair, and beads.

I saw Jesus sneaking around the back street yesterday,
    Lord.
He was sitting on the curb with some greasy char-
    acter in bellbottoms.
They talked a long time and nobody paid much
    attention till they stood up and walked down
    the street together.
It had to be Jesus, Lord, because nobody else would
    bother to take a second look, let alone walk with
    him in public.
Maybe to Jesus that guy is a person
        but
        I confess
    to me he's still a creep.

Get us out of this stained-glass bubble, Lord.

The church has to be in the world, not protected from it.

Help us drain our coffers and spill them over human need until like happy mavericks we can stand with naked consciences.

Help us rip down anything which separates the church from the world, remembering You didn't send Your son to save the church but to save the world.

Keep us from tinkering with world issues until we lie awake to cry with the suffering and crave with the starving.

O God, the world is full of mountains to be moved and we're orbiting them in our stained-glass capsules.

Great Scott, it's a flashing neon cross, Lord.
Is this the last gimmick in our pitch for religiosity?
    Our steeples get higher
      bells fancier
      windows artier
      budgets fatter
        and
      deposit boxes heavier.
Have we lost track of the square carpenter in burlap?

If man isn't careful, Lord, he'll get a gold record
    for hindsight
    for mental antique furniture
    for intellectual trivia
    for the care and feeding of apathy
    for little volleys at brotherhood
    for dehydrating hope
        and
    for fertilizing humanism.
What does one do with a gold record, Lord?
Play it over and over from the beginning?

Who says we're born free—a credit-card company?
  I don't believe it, Lord.
We're tied and tattooed by color
    clubs
      cash
        community
          church
            credit
              and
                chrome.
Nobody is free.
So don't expect us to give away everything and fol-
    low You
        because
we're afraid of withdrawal pains from affluence.

Where do I stand, Lord?
I've got chronic decentralization of my faith.
Ask me again about
        "Who do you say I am?"
This is faith at the stake, Lord. But after all I have
    to believe in my mind what I hope in my heart.

Lord, it's not as hard to love You with all my heart,
    soul, strength, and mind as it is to love my
    neighbor. That's something else.
She lives life on a social Pogo stick and her driveway
    could double as a suburban throughway.
The family is divided by the court and relations are
    knit loosely into his, hers, and theirs.
The neighbors have decided she is a restless native
    who looks like a biological time bomb set for
    countdown.
Nobody would need to tap her phone for information
    because she lives the private life of a goldfish.
Lord, she isn't in need.
She isn't sick.
She isn't weak or heavy laden.
So by your definition is she really my neighbor?
It's easy to pass her by on the other side.

Thank God for ★ ★ ★

O Lord,
    what keeps You from writing off people
        and
    going back to taming the menagerie?

Thank you for the saint I met yesterday in the restaurant, Lord.
I didn't see any misty eyes or halo but while eating steak and french fries he reminded me:
    that world peace is still realistic because man has tremendous capacity for reverence for life,
    that holy communion is possible with coffee and doughnuts as long as it's love in operation,
    that crucifixion may be accomplished over the telephone or back fence as well as on a cross,
    that spiritual renewal may come as a good idea, a new friend, a worthwhile deed, as well as bent knees,
    that the high cost of loving is worth the price-tag.

Help! Help!
There's a storm coming, Lord,
    and
    man is sleeping at the oars.
Everybody knows the boat is leaking
    but
knowing is easier than bailing.
Every wave is higher than the last
    and
    harbor is almost out of sight.
Shake the boat, Lord.
Shake it
    until we wake up and start to row.
Some of us are so asleep we don't even
    know there's danger.

Thank you, God, for hiding secret clocks in unsuspected places to surprise man in his monotonous routine.

How did You ever think of a clock inside the crocus to make it bloom knee-deep in snow

Or the punctuality which rouses a sleeping dog to carry a leash to the front door

Or the timing of a butterfly shedding its swaddling clothes

Or the mysterious picking from inside a twenty-one-day-old egg

Or the split-second timing that triggers an eclipse

Or the alarm that wakes the rooster on a dark winter morning?

It takes man twenty-one jewels and a measure of gold to make a watch

but in Your hands, Lord,

a little dab of miracle will do it.

I believe in investments, Lord, and don't mind ad-
mitting that I'm putting my shekels where they
multiply while I sleep.
But the more shekels I get the less I sleep for fear
they won't multiply.
While interest rates are high I get consumed daily in
reinvesting.
When they are low I'm afraid of too much daily
consuming.
I can't figure whether it's better to
      look rich and think worried
        or
      look worried and think rich.
What did You say we ought to do with our treasures,
Lord?

That woman likes everybody in our office, Lord.
She has walked the second mile around every desk
              and
       has the gift of a built-in hearing aid.
She listens so intently I feel like the whole show
       just telling her about my kids.
If it's a promotion gimmick it's smooth.
If it's for status it may hit a dry run.
If it's for real she's side-kick to an angel.
I think by putting mileage on deeds, Lord,
       she's putting muscles in love.

Lord,
>   to most of us that cantankerous old fool is a mis-
>   sion impossible.
>   He rules the roost by cane and a little bell.
>   If ever anybody needs a personality transplant
>   he does.
>>   But
>   she loves him, Lord, as a daughter should as her
>   father totters toward the finale.
>   I'll bet she puffs pillows and carries tea in her sleep.
>   What is it with love?
>   I thought patient, kind, long-suffering love dropped
>   out in favor of Sunday visiting from 2:00 to 4:00.

Lord, is leaning a part of Your plan?
I notice that
 friends lean in trust,
 nations lean in mutual good faith,
 students lean on past knowledge,
 witnesses for good lean on inner conviction,
 the ill lean on medicine,
 the dying lean on time,
 salvation leans on faith,
 achievement leans on work,
  and
 prayer leans on belief in You.

Lord, following You is too much.
Did You pick me or did I volunteer?
    I've decided
Your rules were wired for pre-moon and
    using them today gives me nothing but static.
    You see
I know the rules but they don't work.
        Not to kill means don't get drafted in the first
        place.
        Not to commit adultery means to ignore so-
        ciety's jolly green giant.
        Honoring parents is only half a rule.
        (What about parents honoring kids?)
        Not telling lies is for the dead.
        Not stealing is for nontaxpayers.
I'm copping out, Lord, and picking up a whole new
    bag.
Did You have to make Your example so spectacular?

Lord,

today as my friend and I spilled ourselves over each other we were, at the same time, filling each other's cup.

I am touched not only by her cascading ideas but the depth at which she wrestles them. To collect ideas is youthful but to wrestle with them is maturity. Most of us have the capacity for wrestling but find it's easier to collect.

People are born collectors, Lord. Each of us is a part of every idea we ever heard, every person we ever knew, every book we ever read, and every experience we ever had. What a collection! But what does it profit us to collect it all and lose the wrestling match with what it means?

I believe that my friend weighs life on a grander scale than most of us. She balances every deed with the heart's intention and shortcoming with a long-range affection. Such a scale not only closes gaps between people but creates a redemptive wholeness.

The time may never come when I find it easy to run the race and not be weary, but being with her today, Lord, gave me the joy of an Emmaus walk.

[47]

God bless her!
During these days sorrow is adding a cubit to her stature and I shade my eyes in the light of her courage.

For most of us grief is a totally opaque experience and we blunder through it with white cane and tin cup promenading our need and reaching for help.

For her grief is re-creative. I hear it in her voice, see it in her eyes, and watch it rub off on others. She has accepted the fact that life ultimately bows to death on the stage of eternity and that You who write the script rotate the cast until each has his turn at stage-center.

Thank You for keeping her from hibernating. Thank You for not allowing her to become desperate. Thank You for not letting her set up a fragile shell of emotion or a crust of bitterness.

Lord, I believe there is a marvelous fellowship of the bereaved, and membership, although freely open, is exclusively understood by those whose broken hearts have been healed by love as they passed through the valley of the shadow.

Lord, I've been thinking about hippies.

Now that my shock absorbers have burst I'm adjusting my antenna for new waves of ideas and culture. There doesn't seem to be much coming in and I'm wondering whether they are a mini-shot of adrenalin or a tribal tragedy.

I am thankful they rattled skeletons in our closet of taboos. Traditions are dangerous. Traditions may be habit instead of right and it's good to knock them before we worship them. Hippies challenged our hangups and some came out sweeter. Others we grumbled over but threw out.

I am thankful too, Lord, that the hippies came on strong. If they hadn't we might not have noticed. After all, the perfumed gladiators were dressed for the occasion and lost to the mob. It was the ragged Christians who made history.

Lord, I feel the hippies are recharging our batteries. Most of us look out through 25-watt eyeballs and miss everything.

Lord, I noticed the halls of ivy are shaking.

This isn't bad, just noteworthy. My rearview mirror
shows me another day when rallies were for
football, pipes were for smoking instead of
climbing into the President's office, and dorms
were unisexed.

Of course it is true that half the campus fizzed up on
week ends and it wasn't always the same half
who flunked out at semester.

Like today, Lord, everybody had his own thing but
nobody got high enough on goldfish to blow
his mind.

Forgive me if I seem cynical, Lord, in observing that
each campus generation has about as much indi-
viduality as a thumbprint but they're all shaped
like the thumb.

They've given him a church in the boondocks, Lord.
I hope he knows that his seminary degree is only a
    learner's permit to take the wheel.
I hope he knows the flock will lean on him for more
    practicing of the Word than preaching it.

Like most apprentices, Lord, he has more tools than
    he can handle.
        Help him be patient.
He has more answers than his flock will have ques-
    tions.
        Help him be forgetful.
He will have more goals than the flock will have
    vision.
        Help him be understanding.
Above all, Lord, nudge him to remember that he is
    not the Master but the servant.
        Help him be loving.

There are a lot of people trying to be good, Lord.
I hope You are giving them credit because most of
us aren't.
You are right. They are like mustard seeds.
They are not scared to death lest they inherit the
earth with its ungovernable cities and bumper-
to-bumper people. They are scared that man's
chronic bewilderment will overpower his po-
tential to conquer these problems.

They do not expect man to become pure in heart
simply by erasing smog from the air. But they
do expect that by Your design the pure in heart
will still be blessed with their promised reward.

They are not comforted by the fact that man is a
social bundle of nerves but are comforted in
that he has unlimited capacity for inner peace
through prayer.

Bless the mustard-seed crop, Lord. It's alive and
living with good vibrations and true grit in every
segment of society.

Lord, have you noticed that charity has gone **into**
      show biz?
It's the revised standard version of
      "help thy neighbor"
        and
      it's tax-deductible.
  (Bigger the stars greater the net receipts
  Higher the tickets greater the social status)
Does it mean, Lord, that human need has grown
      beyond man's level of sensitivity
        or that
      man's level of sensitivity
  is so low it's driving him to pay conscience money
      the painless way?
Something tells me that when we stop crying a river
      over human need we must stop expecting a
      flood of brotherly love.

[53]

Thank God for ★ ★ ★

O *God*, today I'm punching in red again.
That foreman is gonna unravel his tonsils.
I don't mean to make excuses but working two jobs
    divides a man against himself.
        I admit it.
I'm scramblin' for a place in the sun, Lord,
    not another promise in the desert.
I'll let him call me a restless native
        but
    I won't let him call me boy.
I'll let him keep me out of the promised land
        but
    I won't let him keep me in chains.
I'll let him psych me up
        but
    I won't let him turn me off.
I want freedom to live now, Lord,
    and not by handout-to-mouth resuscitation.

What's the point of forgiving everything, Lord?
Or have You stopped blushing like the rest of us?
 We wink at hanky-panky
  soft-pedal sin a-go-go
  tolerate crime
  perpetuate war
   and
  suspect peaceniks.
Why did You forgive the adultress, Lord?
Was it a lesson teaching us to forgive anybody
  anything?
   Or
 teaching us to accept the sinner
   and
  condemn the sin?
That's complicated, Lord, and remember some of us
  in the religious mod squad get confused by
  thinking.

Yes, Lord, I believe in great ideas.
    Doesn't everyone?
But getting them down for use is as hard as carving
    out the Grand Canyon with a teaspoon.
Most of us believe in communication but our image
    of it is talk, talk, talk.
We believe in progress but the possibility of change
    causes a wild dashing back to the good old days.
We believe in cleanliness but scrubbing up the world
    gives us claustrophobia in the pocketbook.
Lord, for best results I suggest that You prestuff
    people with great ideas before their birth day.

O *Lord*, when quietness breaks the habit of my pace
     and
  the press of people is shut outside,
     then
  by the angelus in my heart,
  I begin my celebration of Your presence
     and
  put a seal upon my commitment.